The History Of Prince Lee Boo, Son Of Abba Thulle,King Of The Pelew Islands: Brought To England By Captain Wilson

George Keate

THE

HISTORY

OF

PRINCE LEE BOO,

SON OF ABBA THULLE,

King of the Pelew Islands

BROUGHT TO ENGLAND BY CAPTAIN WILSON,

Commander of the Antelope, East India Packet,

Which was wrecked off these Islands, on her passage, from China,

on the 9th, of August, 1783.

WITH AN ACCOUNT OF

LEE BOO'S DEATH.

And he was buried in Rotherhithe Church-Yard, where a
Tomb is erected to his Memory.

London:

PRINTED FOR THOMAS HUGHES,
35, LUDGATE STREET.

1823.

Plummer and Brewis, Printers, Love-Lane, Eastcheap.

Frontispiece

Rotherithe Church Yard, the
Burial Place of Prince Lee Boo.
Page 103.

Published by T. Hughes. September. 1823.

HISTORY

OF

PRINCE LEE BOO.

———

THE Pelew Islands, one of which gave
birth to the amiable Prince who is the chief
subject of the following pages, are situated in
the western part of the Pacific Ocean; and
were in all probability, first noticed by the
Spaniards of the Philippines, and by them
called the Palos Islands, from the tall Palm-
trees which grow there in great numbers, and
which, at a distance, have the appearance of
masts of ships; the word *palos*, in the Spanish
language, sometimes signifying a mast.

There is every reason to suppose that no
European had ever been upon them, before

the Antelope, a packet belonging to the East
India Company, and commanded by Captain
Henry Wilson, was wrecked there in the night
between the 9th and 10th of August, 1783 : a
misfortune the more distressing to the crew, as
they were utterly ignorant what resources the
Islands afforded, or supposing them to be inhabited, what might be the disposition of the
inhabitants. The perplexities and fears of
such a situation may be better conceived than
described. However, by means of the boats,
and their own vigorous exertions, they reached
land about three or four leagues distant from
the rocks upon which their ship had struck ;
it proved to be an island not constantly inhabited,
but resorted to occasionally by the natives
of some other islands, whom, in the course
of a few days, they found to be a people
simple in their manners, delicate in their
sentiments, and friendly in their dispositions—
a people, in short, who do honour to the
human race.

The opening a communication, as well by
discourse as by good offices, between such a
people and perhaps as meritorious a captain
and crew as ever plouged the main, was effected by a union of singular circumstances. It
happened that a native of Bengal, who spoke
the Malay language perfectly well, had been
recommended to Captain Wilson as a servant
it had also happened that nearly a year before,
a tempest had thrown on those parts, a Malay,
who, as a stranger, had been noticed and
favoured by the king, and who was now become acquainted with the language of the
islanders. By these extraordinary events,
both the English and the inhabitants of Pelew
had each an interpreter, who could converse
freely together in the Malay tongue ; and
Capt. Wilson's servant, whose name was Tom
Rose, speaking English, an easy intercourse
immediately took place on both sides, and all
those impediments were at once removed,
which would have arisen among people having

no way of conveying their thoughts to one
another but by signs and gestures, which might
often have been misunderstood. Thus the
English had the happy opportunity of communicating the particulars of the calamity
which had befallen them, and of imploring the
friendship of the natives; and these, in return,
finding their visitors to have no hostile inten-
tions, freely gave them the good-will they desired; and if but little was in their power,
that little they bestowed generously to relieve
their distress.

The natives themselves were of a deep cop-
per-colour, and naked; and the astonishment
of those, who first discovered the English, on
seeing their colour, plainly shewed that they
had never before beheld a white man. The
clothes of the strangers, too, puzzled them exceedingly; for it seemed to be a matter of
doubt with them, whether those and their
bodies did not form one substance, till the use
and occasion thereof were explained by the

Malay. The same idea, afterwards, prevailed
among others; for when one of the crew (the
Captain's brother) was deputed to wait upon
the king, who resided in an island at some
distance from that whereon they had saved
their lives, he accidentally pulled off his hat, at
which the gazing spectators were all struck
with astonishment, as if they thought it had
formed a part of his head.

. Abba Thulle, which was the king's name,
being a man of great humanity as well as ex
traordinary natural understanding, was no less
affected with the misfortune the English had
met with, than surprised at their persons, and
assured them of his friendship and favour.
He paid them frequent visits, shewing the
utmost admiration at every thing he saw, and
the greatest good-will and regard for them and
their concerns; and granted them permission
to avail themselves of every conyeniency his
country afforded for their relief; for the captain and crew entertained a hope, as the ship

did not go immediately to pieces, of being
enabled, by means of the tools and materials
they might get out of her, to build another
vessel sufficiently large to convey them to
Macao, or some part of China.

As they pursued this design, new wonders
broke upon Abba Thulle and his countryman,
who till now where utter strangers to the forge,
the saw, and other European implements and
utensils; by the use of which they saw such
things performed as impressed them with equal
surprise and esteem—even the grindstone
struck them with wonder; and they could not
look upon the English but as a superior as well
as an uncommon kind of human beings.

But if the king and his people were so surprised at the effect of a saw or grindstone,
what must have been their astonishment at that
of a gun!—To give them some idea of it, on
the first visit from the king, Captain Wilson
ordered his men to be exercised before him
and his numerous attendants, and to fire three

vollies, in different positions; when the surprise
of the natives was well marked by their hollow-
ing, hooting, jumping, and chattering, which
produced a noise almost equal to the report of
the musquets. After this, one of the fowls,
which had been saved from the little live stock
of the Antelope, was purposely driven across the
cove where they were assembled, and where one
of the officers was prepared with a fowling-piece
loaded with shot. He fired, and the bird
instantly dropped, having its wing and leg broken. Some of the natives ran to it, took it up,
and carried it to the king, who examined it with
great attention, unable to understand how it could
be wounded, not having seen any thing pass
out of the gun. This created a vast murmur
and amazement among them.

It is but natural to suppose, after this dis-
play of their power, that the English were
regarded with no small degree of reverence,
and as persons whose friendship and assistance
might be of the greatest advantage to the peo-

ple who had given them so kind a welcome to
their country. All the islands lying in this
spot of the globe, and now known to us by
the name of the Pelew islands, do not belong
to one sovereign; there are several govern-
ments or kingdoms, and one of the greatest
failings in the characters of the different nations consists in that wherein they are like
Europeans—they have wars one with another.
Abba Thulle was then at war with some of his
neighbours. He instantly conceived the great
superiority a few muskets would give him over
his enemies; but his native delicacy rendered
it extremely difficult to make the request. He
had an earnest desire to ask a favour, which
the generosity of his feelings would not allow
him to mention. The English had been, and
still were, in his power: they had sought his
protection as unfortunate strangers—he had
already shewn them, and still meant to shew
them, every mark of hospitality which his
naked unproductive country could afford—he

feared that what he wished to ask, as it might prove a temporary inconvenience, would appear unkind—and what most checked his speaking was, that, circumstanced as the English were, a request would have the appearance of a command.—Reflections which would have done honour to the most enlightened king upon earth !—However, the matter was of the greatest consequence; and at length, after a most severe struggle within himself, the noble Abba Thulle ventured to request that Captain Wilson would permit four or five of his men to accompany him, with their musquets, on an expedition against an island which had done him an injury. The king found the English not ungrateful; the request was willingly complied with, every one of them expressed a readiness to go; but five young men, who were particularly desirous of the appointment, were chosen from the rest.

In the forenoon of the following day, which was the 17th of August, the five Englishmen

attended Abba Thulle, according to his desire,
being distributed in five canoes ; and having
left Oroolong, the name of the island which
had proved so secure an asylum to them,
they were conveyed to another of the king's
islands, at about six leagues distance, where
they were treated with great kindness and
hospitality. They set sail the next morning
for Pelew, the place of the king's residence,
and capital, as we shall call it, of the island of
Coorooraa, about three or four miles farther :
here they remained till the 21st, as the king
could not till then get all his canoes together :
early on that day, however, there was a muster
of them before the king's house, with their
arms, which consisted of Bamboo darts from
five to eight feet long, pointed with the wood
of beetle-nut tree, and bearded ; these are used
for close quarters : but there are short ones
for distance, which are thrown by means of a
stick two feet long. The English again embarked in five different canoes, and sailed away.

about ten or twelve leagues, calling as they
proceeded at several of the king's villages to
refresh and reinforce.   Between two and three
o'clock in the afternoon, they got sight of the
enemy.   They were now with the king 150
canoes, containing considerably more than 1000
men.   The English could not find out the force
of the enemy.

Before any hostilities were commenced, the
king's eldest brother, whose name was Raa
Kook, who was ranked as general of his forces,
went in his canoe close to the town : he had
with him one of the Englishmen, who, however, was ordered not to fire till a certain signal
should be given for that purpose.   The general
talked with the enemy for some time; but what
he said being received with great indifference,
he threw a spear at them, which they almost
instantly returned.   This being the signal for
firing, was immediately obeyed—a man was
seen to fall, and this threw the enemy into great
confusion.   Such as were on shore ran away,

and the greater part of those in the canoes, jumped into the water, and made for land. A few more muskets were fired, which entirely dispersed the enemy. Thus successful, Abba Thulle thought proper to return with his fleet of canoes, and safely sent back his English allies to Oroolong, after having expressed great satisfaction at their behaviour, treated them in the best manner he could, and promised supplies of provisions for their companions. Indeed, the whole country resounded with their praises; and within a few days the king actually gave Captain Wilson the island of Oroolong for the English.

Who can wonder that Abba Thulle should take advantage of the opportunity (which now offered) of bringing all his enemies to his own terms? Accordingly we find, that a few days afterwards, he requested ten men from Captain Wilson, to go on another expedition against the enemy. This second request of Abba Thulle was as readily granted as the former, and ten men were chosen.

The king, attended by upwards of 200 canoes, proceeded in the night-time towards Artingal, off which island the fleet arrived a little before day-break, but then halted till the rising of the sun, it being a maxim with the natives of Pelew never to attack an enemy in the dark, or take him by surprise. As the day came on, a small canoe, containing only four men, each with a white feather stuck up in his hair, was dispatched with a message to the enemy, who, observing this signal of parley, dispatched a canoe to Raa Kook for that purpose. Raa Kook demanded whether they would submit to such terms as his brother had proposed, by way of atoning for injuries complained of. To this demand, after communicating it to the king of Artingal, the enemy's canoe brought back a flat refusal; upon which Abba Thulle ordered his conch-shell to be sounded, and made the signal for his canoes to arrange themselves in order of battle.

This expedition ended with the loss to the

enemy of six canoe and nine prisoners, which
to them was great, a canoe being esteemed as
much consequently as the largest man of war
in Europe.

Still, however, the people of Artingal refused to submit; and a third expedition, more
formidable than the others, was soon afterwards resolved upon, in which Abba Thulle
was not only accompanied by ten of the
English, but had also a swivel gun. The
number of canoes, which now attended the
king, far exceeded those he had before, he
being assisted, on this occasion, by his neighbouring allies. But the people of Artingal
declined fighting upon the water; so that
Abba Thulle's forces landed and attacked
them on shore. The swivel played constantly
upon the houses, which were filled with
people; and the English musketry, covering
the Pelew people, soon dislodged the enemy.

In this action five canoes were destroyed,
which the enemy had hauled on shore, and

much other damage done : but what was the
greatest matter of triumph to the people of
Pelew was, their carrying away the stone
whereon the king of Artingal used to sit in
council ; which probably, was with them
reckoned as glorious an exploit, as that of
Edward the First's bringing to England the
stone on which the kings of Scotland used to
be crowned, which is now in Westminster
Abbey in London. Indeed, finding it in vain to
contend against such evident advantages as the
people of Pelew derived from their English
auxiliaries, the king of Artingal very prudently dropped the war, and concluded a peace.

In this battle a son of Raa Kook, about
18 years of age, was slain. He had been
wounded in the second action by a spear flung
into his foot, and the natives, in trying to pull
it out, had broken it short off. Mr. Sharp
the surgeon, had been sent by Captain Wilson
to cure the wound in his foot, and had brought
his surgical instruments with him for that

purpose: he arrived in Pelew however, only
to witness the ceremony of his funeral. On
his arrival Raa Kook carried him to a neighbouring island ; there after a repast, which
was eat in the most profound silence, the
lamentation of women was heard at some distance, and Mr. Sharp going to see the occasion
of it, on a sign from his conductor, observed a
great number of them following a dead body
on a bier, tied up in a mat, and supported on
the shoulders of four men, who were the only
ones present. The body was then deposited
in a grave, without any ceremony, except that
the lamentations of the women continued.
Raa Kook, it is remarkable, never gave the
smallest hint or indication that this was the
funeral of his son.

The surprise and pleasure of the king,
on examining the instruments, were very great;
and there being some stranger chiefs residing
with him, on account of his late success, he
begged that they also might be gratified with

a sight of them.   An explanation of the different
uses to which they could be put, excited much
amazement.

Not long afterwards, Abba Thulle took
occasion once more to beg the assistance of the
English on an expedition against another
island, named Pelelew, and ten men were
lent him as before.   On this enterprise he was
attended by full 300 canoes.   Upon their
arrival off Pelelew; the enemy thought proper, after receiving some damage on a neighbouring island, to sue for peace, to which no
doubt, they were chiefly induced by the terror
of the English fire-arms.   Two Malays, who
had been wrecked with the one already mentioned as the interpreter between the English
and the people of Pelew, were, at its conclusion,
given up to Abba Thulle.

It was now the latter end of October; and
such of the crew of the Antelope as had
not accompanied Abba Thulle on his expe-
ditions, having been indefatigable in getting

stores and planks from the ship, in cutting
down timber on the island, and in forwarding,
by every means in their power, the grand
object in view, they had the satisfaction to
hope, from the great progress they had made,
that success would attend their endeavours,
and that they should soon complete such a
vessel, as would carry them to Macao, or some
part of China, as before mentioned; and this
encouraged them to persevere in their labours,
however toilsome, with cheerfulness and alacrity.

Abba Thulle was always approached by
his rupacks or chiefs, with the greatest respect;
and his common subjects whenever they passed near him, put their hands behind them,
and crouched towards the ground.. The eyes
of all beheld their naked prince with as much
respect and awe as those are viewed who rule
polished nations, and are surrounded with all
the splendour of royalty.' 'Whether in council,
or elsewhere,' when any message came from the
king, if it was brought by one of the common

people, it was delivered at some distance in a low voice, to one of the inferior rupacks, who, bending in an humble posture at the king's side, repeated the message in a soft tone, with his face turned away. On the king's part, his behaviour was, on all occasions, gentle and gracious. Every day in the afternoon, whether he was at Pelew, or with the English at Oroolong, he sat in public, for the purpose of hearing requests, or of settling differences which might have arisen among his subjects; and having heard whatever they had to say to him, by his affability and condescension he never suffered them to depart dissatisfied. He reigned over them more as the father than the sovereign. His commands appeared to be absolute, yet he never undertook any thing of importance without advising with his rupacks in council; this was always held in the open air, on a large square pavement, each rupack sitting on a single stone, and the king upon one more elevated than the rest, with another close to it for the occasional support of his arm.

Next in power to the king was Raa Kook, the brother next to him by birth, and, by the custom there, general of all his forces, and heir to the throne, the government of Pelew not going to the king's children till it has passed through the hands of his brothers.

A particular chief, or rupack, constantly attended the king, apparently as his minister. He was always first consulted, but never bore arms.

The rupacks, or chiefs, may be considered in the same light as the European nobles. With respect to property in these islands, a man's house or canoe is considered as his own, as is also the land allotted him, as long as h occupies and cultivates it; but, whenever he removes with his family to another place, the ground becomes again the property of the king, who gives it to whom he pleases, or to those who ask permission to cultivate it.

The country is well covered with timber trees, the trunk of one of which furnishes the natives with canoes, some large enough to carry thirty-men: there are but few other trees of much use to the natives.

Yams and cocoa-nuts, being their chief article of food, are attended to with the utmost care. Amongst his crew, Capt. Wilson had some Chinese, which people are all tolerable botanists, and will pick up a meal almost any where. He sent one of them about the country, to see what productions he could meet with; his report, on his return, was as follows:

"*This is very poor place, and very poor peo-*" "*ple; no got clothes, no got rice, no got hog, no*" "*got nothing only yams, little fish, and cocoa-*" "*nut; no got nothing make trade, very little*" "*make eat.*"—

This account, however, is too unfavourable; there are a few pigeons (which are reserved for people of a certain dignity,) and plenty of cocks and hens, though till informed by the English, the natives knew not that these last were good to eat; and the sea affords a variety

of fish. No four footed animal was found here,
except some wild brownish gray rats. From
the scanty produce of the country, it is plain
no luxury can reign amongst the inhabitants
in their diet; and the milk of the cocoa-nut
was their common drink: on particular occasions, they added to their ordinary fare certain
sweetmeats and sweet drink, obtained by the
aid of a syrup, extracted either from the palm-
tree or the sugar-cane.

The houses are raised about three feet from
the ground, the foundation beams being laid
on large stones, whence spring the upright
supports of their sides, which are crossed by
other timbers grooved together, and fastened
by wooden pins, the intermediate spaces being
closely filled up with bamboos and palm-trees
platted together. As to domestic implements,
they are little baskets, very nicely woven from
slips of the plantain-leaf ; and wooden baskets
with covers, neatly carved and inlaid with
shells. No one ever stirs abroad without a

basket, which usually contains some beetle-nut,
a comb, a knife, and a little twine. The best
knives are made of a piece of the large mother-
of-pearl oysters, ground narrow, and the outward side a little polished. Combs are made
from the orange-tree (of which there are a few
of the Seville kind,) the handle and teeth
fashioned in the solid wood. The fishing hooks
are of tortoise-shell; and twine, cord, and
fishing nets are well manufactured from the
husks of a cocoa-nut. Of the plantain-leaf
are formed mats, which serve the people as
beds. They also use a plantain-leaf at meals
instead of a plate, and the shell of a cocoa-nut
supplies the place of a cup.

The natives, in general, are a stout well-made
people, rather above the middling stature, and
of a very deep copper colour, but not black
Their hair is long, and generally formed into
one large loose curl round their heads. The
men are entirely naked; the women wear two
little aprons, one before, the other behind.

D

Both men and women are tatooned ; and their
teeth blackened by a preparation of groundsel
and some other herbs, the application of which
makes them for a time extremely sick. In
the gristle between their nostrils is bored a
hole, through which they often put any little
sprig or blossom which happens to strike their
fancy. Both sexes also, are very expert at
swimming; and the men such admirable divers,
that they will readily fetch up any thing which
attracts their notice—The conduct of these
people towards the English was, from first to
last, uniformly courteous and attentive, accompanied with a politeness which surprised those
who were the objects of it. They felt our countryman were distressed, and in consequence,
wished them to share whatever they had to give.
The English had also many opportunities of
observing that this liberality prevailed in all the
intercourse the natives had among themselves.
The tenderness shown to the women was remarkable, and the deportment of the men to each other,

mild and affable; insomuch that, in the various
scenes of which they were spectators, the English
never saw any thing which had the appearance
of quarrelling or passion; every one seemed to
attend to his own concerns, without interfering
with the business of his neighbour; herein
giving an example which ought to put to the
blush many a gossiping busy body in our own
country. . Raa Kook and Arra Kooker, brothers to the king, were amongst the natives,
who first discovered the English on the island
of Oroolong after their being wrecked, and
who immediately conceived the greatest affection and friendship for them. Raa Kook
seemed to be about forty years of age, was of
a middling height, rather corpulent, and had a
countenance marked with great sense and good
nature.—As the elder brother, he was the
king's next heir, and general of the forces. His
character was firm and resolute, yet full of
humanity : he was steady and persevering in
whatever he undertook : he delivered his or-

ders to the people with the greatest mildness, yet would be obeyed : and they, as if mingling affection with duty, never failed to serve him with alacrity and ardour. Whilst on one hand, the rank of this amiable chief enabled him to be of essential service to the English : on the other, he shewed perfect satisfaction and pleasure in whatever they did for him : he delighted in their company, and courted their information, for he had an eager spirit of enquiry, was very minute in. his observations, desired to examine the nature of every thing he saw, and understood whatever was described to him, with the greatest ease and quickness. He was always pleasant and lively, well disposed to laughter when it was occasionally excited, and sometimes excited it himself. Having once been presented with a pair of trowsers and an uniform coat, he immediately put them on, not a little pleased in appearing like his new acquaintance, often looking at himself and calling out, " Raa Kook Engles !

Raa Kook Engles!" He would sit at table
as they did, instead of squatting on his hams,
(as is the custom of the country), and endeavour to accommodate himself to their manners
in all respects. In short, they felt great regard for him from the first, and in truth found
him in every transaction they afterwards had
with him, to be a man of an upright character
and steady friendship.

Arra Kooker was nearly forty years of age,
of the middle size and so plump and fat, that
he was almost as broad as he was long. He
possessed a fund of humour, and a particular
turn for mimicry. He could by no means
relish wearing trowsers, but conceiving a passion for a white shirt, one was accordingly
given to him: this he had no sooner put on,
than he began to dance and jump about with
so much glee, that all were highly diverted by
his ridiculous gestures, and the contrast which
the colours of the linen formed with that of his
skin. He would frequently amuse our coun-

trymen by taking off every one of them in any
particularity he had noticed; and sometimes
would put a hat on his head, and imitate the
manner of their walking in their military exercise; and nothing that he observed done by
them escaped him. The English had saved
from the Antelope, a large Newfoundland dog,
named Sailor, which afforded equal surprise
and delight to all the natives who saw him,
and they often used to divert themselves by
making him bark. Arra Kooker was accus-
tomed to carry him victuals, whence the dog
naturally expressed great joy on seeing him;
and the humorous prince would often add to
his other amusements by imtiating wonderfully
well the barking, howling, jumping, and all
various tokens of joy of this useful animal.—
Indeed, he grew so fond of Sailor, that on his
earnest and repeated entreaties, the creature
was at last given to him.

So unremitting had the English worked on
the vessel which was to be the means of their

deliverance, that by the 9th of November it
was ready for launching, and this being hap-
pily accomplished, they began to put on board
every thing which they judged would be necessary to them in their voyage. By Abba
Thulle's desire she was called the Oroolong.

Throughout the whole progress of building
the vessel, the king had in his visits to the
English, been very attentive to their manner
of working; he would stand looking at them
for a considerable time together, and let not
the most trifling circumstance escape his observation. He was now come to Oroolong with
some of his chiefs, to be present at their departure. In the evening of the day after the
vessel was launched, he entered very seriously
into conversation with Captain Wilson: he
said, that, notwithstanding he was looked up
to by his subjects with respect, and regarded
as their superior as well in knowledge as his
rank, yet, after mixing with the English, and
being witness of their ingenuity, he was often

conscious of his own insignificance, in beholding
the meanest of them exercise talents to which he
had ever been a stranger : and that therefore, after
due consideration, he had come to the resolution
of committing his second son, whose name was

LEE BOO,

to the captain's care, in order that he might
enjoy the advantage of improving himself by
accompanying the English, and also of learning many, things, which, on his return, might
prove of essential benefit to his country.   He
then spoke of his son as a youth of gentle and
amiable disposition, sensible, and possessing
many good qualities.   He said, he had recalled
him from a distant place where he had been
under the care of an old man : that he was at
that time taking leave of his friends at Pelew,
and would come to Oroolong the next day.
He added, that one of the Malays from Pelew
should accompany him as a servant.   Raa
Kook and Arra Kooker joined in commenda-
tion of their nephew.

To this address of the king's, Captain Wilson answered, that he was exceedingly honoured and obliged by the singular mark of confidence and esteem he had mentioned; that he should have considered himself bound in gratitude to take care of any person belonging to Pelew whom he might think proper to send; but, in the case proposed, he wished solemnly to assure him, that he should endeavour to merit the high trust reposed in him, by treating the young prince with the same affection and tenderness as his own son.—It was evident that answer gave the king great satisfaction.

After this, the discourse of the day, as might be expected, turning much on the departure of the English, Abba Thulle addressed Captain Wilson, as they sat together, as follows: " You " are going, and, when gone, I fear the in- " habitants of Artingal will come down in " great numbers, and molest me, as they have " done frequently before; and having lost the " aid of the English, I shall be unable to re-

" sist them, unless you leave me a few of your
" muskets, which you have already taught me
" to hope you would."

As a testimony of the gratitude the crew
owed this worthy man, and as a means of ren-
dering him service after their departure, by
arming him against his enemies, it had been
intended to leave with Abba Thulle, on quitting the island, whatever fire-arms they could
spare: on this request, therefore, they now
presented him, in addition to some working
tools and other things they had given him
before, five muskets, five cutlasses, a barrel of
gunpowder, and gun-flints, and ball in pro-
portion; to which Captain Wilson added his
own fowling-piece, wherewith his royal friend
seemed to be particularly pleased, having often
been witness of its effects.

At the same time that Abba Thulle had
been meditating upon the design of sending
his son LEE Boo to England, that of remaining behind with the natives had been formed

by one of the English seamen, whose name was Madan Blanchard: a design in whch, however extraordinary it may seem, he persisted, notwithstanding the Captain used many arguments to persuade him to drop it. At length, finding it in vain to alter his resolution, the Captain judged it prudent to let him follow his own inclination. Captain Wilson took an opportunity of imparting the matter to the king in the manner he had proposed, with which he was so well pleased that he promised, on Blanchard's being introduced, to give him a house and plantations, and to make him a rupack.

In the evening of the 11th of November, LEE Boo arrived at Oroolong, and was introduced by his father, first to Capt. Wilson, and then to his officers. He approached them all in so easy and affable a manner, and with such an expression of sense and good humour in his countenance, that every one immediately became prepossessed in his favour, and felt the

commencement of that regard for him, which
his amiable manners daily increased. He was
brought by his elder brother, whose name was
Qui Bill; a youth about 21 years of age, extremely well made, but who had lost his nose,
which might have been accidently carried off
in battle by a spear, or destroyed by what we
call the Evil, a disorder which the surgeon of
the Antelope, Mr. Sharp, found to prevail
among the natives.

With Lee Boo was brought from Pelew, a
basket, containing some dozens of fruit resem-
bling an apple, of an oblong shape and a deep
crimson colour, somewhat like what is called
in England, the Dutch Paradise Apple. This
fruit was spoken of as very rare, and just then
coming into season. Captain Wilson gave one
of the apples to each of his officers, being such
as they had not seen before: the rest he carefully reserved to treat his young passenger
with, during his voyage.

Every requisite being now put on board the

E

The Cordura and of the XXXII having the Matter Cornwall.

vessel, and the wind fair, the next day was
appointed by the Captain, for the affecting
scene of bidding a last adieu to those friendly
islanders, to whom he and his crew were so
much indebted, and who much wished for
their longer stay: but the Captain was fearful
of not reaching China soon enough to secure a
passage in some of the English ships on their
return to Europe that season. Abba Thulle,
therefore lost no time; he entered into long
discourse with his son; giving him instructions
how to conduct himself, and what he was to
attend to; and telling him, amongst many
other good councils, that he was thence-forward
to consider Capt. Wilson as another father,
and win his affections, by observing his advice.
Here turning to the Captain, he said, " When
" Lee Boo got to England, he would have
" such fine things to see, that he might chance
" to slip away from him to run after novelty;
" but that he hoped the captain would keep
" him as much as he could under his eye, and

" endeavour to moderate the eagerness of his
" youth."

And after further conversation relative to the
confidence placed in him, the unlettered king
of Coorooraa concluded his recommendation,
nearly in the following expressions, which must
make their way to the hearts of every reader of
the least sensibility : " I would wish you,
" said he to Capt. Wilson, to inform LEE BOO
" of all things which he ought to know, and
" make him an Englishman.—The object of
" parting with my son I have frequently
" thought on; I am well aware, that the dis-
" tant countries he must go through, differing
" much from his own, may expose him to dan-
" gers, as well as to diseases that are unknown
" to us here, in consequence of which he may
" die ;—I have prepared my thoughts to
" this;—I know that death is to all men in-
" evitable, and whether my son meets this
" event at Pelew or. elsewhere, is immaterial.
" I am satisfied from what I have observed of

" the humanity of your character, that, if he
" is sick, you will be kind to him; and should
" that happen, which your utmost care cannot
" prevent, let it not hinder you, or your bro-
" ther, or your son, or any other of your
" countryman, returning here; I shall receive
" you, or any of your people, in friendship,
" and rejoice to see you again."

Who is not struck with this proof of the
great strength of Abba Thulle's understanding,
as well as the purity and liberality of his
sentiments?

Captain Wilson repeated his assurance, that
he would take the same care of LEE BOO as
of his own child, and that nothing should be
wanting on his part to shew, in his attention to
the son, the gratitude and regard he should
ever feel for the father.

The time of departure being so near, the
captain took an opportunity of conversing
with Blanchard on the subject of his being left behind. He set before him the man

ner in which he should conduct himself towards the natives, and in what respects he could be instructive and beneficial to them. He very prudently counselled him never to go naked like the natives, as, by adhering to the form of dress his countrymen had appeared in, he would always maintain a superiority of character; and that he might the better follow this advice, Blanchard was furnished with all the clothes that could be spared, and directed, when those were worn out, to make himself trowsers of a mat, which he could always get from the natives, and thereby preserve that decency he had always been used to. Nor did the captain forget, in his instructions, to recommend an attention to religious matters. He urged Blanchard, in the most earnest manner not to neglect those acts of devotion which he had been taught to practice, but carefully to observe the Sabbath-day.

In the morning of the 12th of November, one of the swivel guns which had been saved

from the wreck, was fired, and an English jack
hoisted at the mast-head of the vessel, as a
signal for sailing, which being explained to the
king, he forthwith ordered to be taken on
board, yams, cocoa-nuts, sweetmeats, and other
things provided for the voyage: besides which
there was a quantity of provisions in many
canoes, belonging to the natives, lying along-
side of the Oroolong.

When the vessel was loaded with as many
of the friendly offerings as could with any
conveniency be taken on board, and got quite
ready for sea, the boat was sent for the captain,
who was on shore. This circumstance being
made known to the king, he signified, that he
and his son would presently go on board in
his canoe. Then the captain, taking Blanchard,
and the men who had come on shore for him,
into one of the temporary houses, besought the
former, to impress on his memory the advice he
had before given him, and particularly to be
observant of his duty to his Creator, that the

people of Pelew might there perceive he re-
tained that faith and sense of religion in which
he had been brought up. In conclusion, the
captain made the seamen present, kneel down
with him, and unite in praises and thanksgiving
to that Supreme Being, who had not only
graciously supported their spirits in the midst
of severe toils and dangers, but had now opened to them the means of deliverance. Abba
Thulle and his chiefs who were near the en-
trance of the house, observed and understood
the meaning of this act of devotion, and pre-
served a profound silence.

At eight o'clock in the morning, the captain
went on board in his boat; and soon afterwards
was followed by the king, his son LEE BOO,
and such rupacks as were with him. The
little vessel was so deeply laden with sea-stores,
that a doubt arose, whether she could be got
over the reef which had proved fatal to the
Antelope, and runs along the west side of the
Pelew islands; it was therefore determined to

lighten her, by landing two six pounders they
had on board.

Mr. Sharp, the surgeon, who, as the person
whose profession it was to cure diseases, had
particularly attracted the king's notice, had
been desired to take LEE Boo under his special care till the Oroolong should arrive at
China; and Abba Thulle now pointed out
that gentleman to his son, as his *succalic*, that
is, particular friend; and from that moment
LEE Boo attached himself to him, keeping
close at his side, in whatever part of the vessel
he went.

In adjusting and setting all things to rights
before the Oroolong moved, a small sail belonging to the pinnace was missed. Blanchard
was got into that boat, in order to take the
Oroolong in tow. He had kept his word;
with unwearied assiduity he had to the last
given his countrymen every assistance in his
power, and, having carefully laid up the sail
enquired after, went on board to shew where.

he had put it; which being done, he wished
them a prosperous voyage, and however
strange it may seem, without discovering the
least degree of regret, took leave of all his old
shipmates with as little appearance of concern
as if they had been only about to sail from
London to Gravesend, to come back with the
next tide.

At length the Orolong was put in motion,
and advanced towards the reef. Loaded as
she had been by Abba Thulle's bounty, even
to excess, with every thing he though might
be useful or agreeable to his departed friends,
still on each side of her were a multitude of
canoes full of the common natives, who had
all brought presents from themselves, entreating
they might be accepted. In vain were they
told there was no room in the vessel for any
thing more; each held up a little something—
" Only this from me! Only this from me!"
was the general cry: which was repeated with
such supplicating countenances and tearful eyes,

that this additional mark of generosity and
affection almost got the better of every body
on board. A few yams or cocoa-nuts were
accepted from some of the nearest: and those
poor creatures whose entreaties could not be
listened to, unable to endure the disappoint-
ment, paddled a head, and threw their little
presents into the pinnace; not knowing that
she was to return with Blanchard.

Can this picture of pure friendship at Pelew
be surpassed by any other in the known
world?

A head of the pinnace went several canoes,
to mark the safest track for the vessel; and
others were stationed at the reef to point out
the deepest water for her passage over it, by
which precautions the Oroolong safely and
easily cleared that formidable barrier.

Abba Thulle accompanied the English in
their vessel almost to the reef, before he made
the signal for his canoe to come along-side.
And now, wishing him happy and prosperous,

he most affectionately took leave of LEE BOO,
and gave him his blessing—it was received
with profound respect. Seeing Captain Wilson
engaged in giving some directions to his people, he stopped till he was perfectly at liberty;
then went up to him, and embraced him with
the greatest tenderness, showing by his voice
and looks, how distressed he was to bid him
farewell. In the most cordial manner he
shook hands with all the officers, saying,
" You are happy because you are going
" home—I am happy to find you are happy—
" but still very unhappy myself to see you
" are going away." Then assuring the crew
of his ardent wishes for their successful voyage,
he went over the side of the vessel into his
canoe. As the canoes drew together, surrounding that of the king, the natives all eagerly
looked up as if to bid adieu, while their countenances showed the feeling of their benevolent
hearts in looks far more expressive than language. The English might truly say that

they left a whole people in tears; indeed so
deeply were they themselves affected by this
interesting scene, that when Abba Thulle and
his attendants turned back to Oroolong, they
were scarcely able to give him three cheers; and
their eyes followed him to catch the latest look,
whilst every man among them with gratitude
felt the extent of his services, whereby, in a
great measure, their deliverance had been
brought about, as well as the sincerity of his
friendship, which had continued firm and unshaken to the last.

Most of the chiefs had left the Oroolong with
the king, except Raa Kook, and a few of his
attendants, who would see her clear out of danger, to the outside of the reef. The outside of
the reef had been some time attained, Raa
Kook had remained pensive, and the vessel
proceeded a considerable way, before he recollected himself and summoned his canoes to
return.—The pinnace being now brought to
the side of the Oroolong, the captain and offi-

cers prepared themselves to take leave of this
amiable person, but when the moment of sepa-
ration arrived he was so effected that for a
short time he was unable to speak—he took
them by the hand, and pointing with the
other to his heart, said *it was there he felt the
pain* of bidding them farewell: nor was this
scene witnessed by any one on board who did
not share its distress. He addressed Lee Boo,
by name, and said a few words to him; but
finding he could not proceed, he went into the
boat, when immediately quitting the rope, he
gave those he had just left a last affectionate
look, then dropped astern.

This worthy chief would fain have accompanied our people to England, and before
their vessel was launched, had actually asked
the king's permission so to do; but, from the
circumstance of his being heir to the crown,
the inconvenience which would arise in case of
Abba Thulle's death in his absence, was a
prudential reason, that prevented its being

granted. Raa Kook's good sense convinced him of the justness of it, and he yielded—but his wish remained the same. To this their first and truly valuable friend, the English presented a brace of pistols, and a cartridge-box loaded with the proper cartridges, at their last interview.

Having now parted from all their friends of Pelew, the crew pursued their voyage towards China, with tolerable weather. The first night LEE Boo slept on board, he ordered his Malay servant, whose name was Boyam, to bring his mat upon deck; a warmer covering was, however, prepared to defend him against the cold. The next morning, no land was to be seen, which much surprised him. Captain Wilson now clothed him in a shirt, waistcoat, and pair of trowsers, the two first articles of which seemed to be very uneasy to him, and he soon took those off, folded them up, and used them only as a pillow; but understanding the indelicacy of having no clothing, he never

F

appeared without his trowsers; and as the
vessel, by steering northward, advanced into a
climate gradually becoming colder, he felt less
and less inconvenience in resuming the use of
his jacket and shirt, and the dislike he had to
them lost itself in his new taught sense of propriety, which daily increasing, soon became
too powerful to suffer him to change his dress
in the presence of another person; and he
would afterwards always retire for that purpose
to some dark corner where he could not be
seen.—At first, the motion of the vessel made
him sea-sick, insomuch that he was obliged
frequently to lie down. On his growing better, one of the apples, which was brought to
Oroolong, at the time of his arrival there, was
given him: he hesitated to eat it, till he was
told that such was the captain's desire, and
that Abba Thulle had sent them for him;
when he observed to Boyam, his servant, that
he was much indulged, as none but a few
great people had his father's permission to eat

of this fruit. This remark corresponds with Abba Thulle's telling Captain Wilson, on giving him these apples, that they were a great rarity.

On the 16th of November, being Sunday, prayers were devoutly read in the forenoon, upon deck, the crew having too deep a sense of the mercies of Providence in their happy delivery, not to offer them publicly and with hearts full of gratitude.

Lee Boo was remarkably clean in his person, washing himself several times every day.—There is a saying of great importance and well worthy of attention, that "cleanliness is next to godliness." It may not be estimating cleanliness too highly to regard it, as being no less essential to the health of the body, than godliness is to that of the soul. However, no one can pretend not to admire and prefer it to filthiness, which yet so much more prevails, especially amongst the poorer class of people; but, surely, this is the result

of a sluggish indolent habit, rather than of
necessity, as, though clothed in rags, they may
be *clean*.

Our young voyager was by this time so well
recovered as to eat a flying-fish which was
caught upon deck, and some yam, having
before eaten very little. He told Boyam, that
he was sensible his father and family had been
very unhappy from knowing that he had been
sick. When he was quite recovered from his
illness he appeared to be perfectly easy and
contented.

In the morning of the 25th, at day-light, the
vessel came in sight of the Bashee Islands at
about three leagues distance. LEE BOO was
much pleased at the circumstance, and eagerly
desired to know their names: which being repeated to him until he could pronounce them,
he took a piece of line, and tied a knot in it in
remembrance of the event. It is the custom of
the people in the Pelew Islands to make remarks
by tying knots in a line, and LEE BOO had

brought with him the one he now used for that purpose.

Having pursued their course without interruption, on Friday the 28th, the voyagers saw several Chinese fishing-boats, and, next morning, land: they stood in amongst the islands, as the wind would permit, till six o'clock in the evening; when they anchored in the midst of some small Chinese vessels; LEE BOO being quite delighted with viewing the land, and the number of boats upon the water.

On the 30th in the morning, Captain Wilson procured a pilot to conduct their vessel between the islands to Macao, where lived Mr. M'Intyre, a gentleman from whom the captain had received many marks of friendship, when before at that place in the Antelope.

To him, therefore, Captain Wilson repaired upon his arrival.————Mr. M'Intyre was was no sooner informed of the sad misfortune which had befallen his friend, than with his usual generosity, he ordered such provisions and other necessaries as they might stand in need of to be sent on board the vessel to the officers and people, whilst the captain wrote to the East India Company's Agents who wer then all at Canton, to acquaint them with his his situation.

Lee Boo was astonished on seeing the Portuguese ships at Macao: he cried out as he looked at them, *Clow, clow, muc, clow!* that is, *Large, large, very large!* The English had here an opportunity of observing the natural benevolence of his mind. Some Chinese boats, rowed by poor Tartar women, with their little children tied to their backs surrounding the vessel, and the poor creatures in them petitioning for fragments of victuals, Lee Boo was very anxious to relieve their necessities, giving them oranges, and selecting, with particular attention from such things as he had, whatever he liked best himself.

The next morning, Mr. M'Intyre and a Portuguese gentleman accompanied the cap-

on board the Oroolong, taking with them a
variety of refreshments and provisions ready
dressed. In the evening, they returned on
shore, together with LEE BOO, and all the
officers, except the chief mate, who remained
with the men to take care of the vessel.

The Portuguese gentleman was very much
pleased with the Pelew Prince, and when on
shore requested that the *new man*, as he called
him, might be permitted to visit his family:
and his house being the first the young travel-
ler had ever entered, he seemed to be lost
in silent admiration. The upright walls and
flat ceilings greatly perplexed him, as he did
not understand how they could be formed;
and the ornaments of the rooms also struck
him with no small degree of astonishment.
On being introduced to the ladies of the family,
his deportment was so easy and polite, as to be
exceeded only by his abundant good nature;
he was not in the least embarrassed: he allowed
the company to examine his hands, which

were tatooed, and appeared pleased with the
notice he excited.

The idea conceived by those who were
witnesses of Lee Boo's first introduction to
fashionable life, was, that how great soever the
surprise, which the scenes of a new world
might occasion in him, it would be scarcely exceeded by that, which his own amiable manners and native polish would create in others.

After this visit, Mr. M'Intyre conducted
Captain Wilson and his companions to his own
house, where they were ushered into a large
hall, lighted up, with a table in the middle covered for supper, and a sideboard very hand-
somely ornamented. A new scene now burst
at once on Lee Boo's mind: he was all eyes,
all admiration: the vessels of glass were in a
manner enchantment itself. Mr. M'Intyre
pointed out to him whatever he thought likely
to amuse him; but every thing around him
was attracting; his eye and his mind were
alike engaged: in truth, all was to him a fairy

tale, a scene of wonder. At the upper end of the hall was a large looking-glass, which reflected almost his whole person. Here LEE BOO stood in perfect amazement at seeing himself— he laughed,—he drew back—he returned to look again, quite lost in wonder. He tried to look behind, as if conceiving somebody to be there, but found the glass fixed close to the wall. Upon this, Mr. M'Intyre ordered a small glass to be brought, wherein having seen his face, LEE Boo looked behind to discover the person who looked at him, totally unable to account for so strange an effect.

After passing an evening rendered pleasant and cheerful by the hospitality of their host, and the simplicity of LEE BOO, the gentlemen retired for the night; whether the prince passed it in sleep, or in thinking upon the occurrences of the preceding day, is not certain; but it is very possible, the next morning, he recollected them in that confused manner, in which we recall something that we have seen in a dream.

The following day, Lee Boo had more leisure for examination: the upright walls and flat ceilings were still objects of surprise to him: the walls he was continually feeling, as if by that means to acquire some idea of their construction; but the ceilings, self-supported as he imagined, seemed, at that time, quite beyond the reach of his comprehension.

By the goods offices of Mr. M'Intyre, a house, servants, and other necessaries were provided at Macao, for the crew of the Oroo-long, and they all came on shore, leaving a guard of one officer and a few men, who at due times were changed. In purchasing such things as they stood in need of, they did not forget Lee Boo, who was a favourite with them all. Among other trinkets, which, from their novelty, they thought would please him, was a string of large glass beads, the sight whereof threw him almost into an ecstacy: he hugged them with a transport which could not be equalled by that of the possessor of a string

of pearls of the same size—he thought he had
in his hands all the wealth the world could
afford—he ran with eagerness to Captain
Wilson to shew him his riches, and enraptured
with the idea of his family's sharing them with
him, in the utmost agitation of spirits, entreated the Captain " immediately to get him a
" Chinese vessel, to carry his treasures to
" Pelew, and deliver them to the king, that he
" might distribute them as he thought proper,
" and thereby see what a country the English
" had conveyed him to;" adding, " that the
" people who carried them should inform the
" king that LEE BOO would soon send him
" other presents." He then assured Captain
Wilson, that, " if the people faithfully exe-
" cuted their charge, he would, besides what
" Abba Thulle might give them, present them,
" on their their return, with one or two beads
" as a reward for their fidelity."—Happy
state of simplicity and innocence, whose plea-
sures can be purchased on such easy terms!

In a short time, Captain Wilson received
letters from the officers of the East India Company at Canton, expressing their concern for
the misfortune of the crew, and advising the
disposal of the vessel and stores. These letters
were accompanied with warm clothes, and a
variety of other necessaries. Mr. M'Intyre
received letters also, desiring him to furnish
them with money, &c.

At Macao, LEE BOO had frequent opportunities of seeing people of different nations;
in particular, the English women, who were
waiting there for a passage to Europe, and
whom he preferred to any other of the fair sex
he had seen.

Their being no four footed animals at Pelew,
(excepting the rats already mentioned,) the
Newfoundland dog, and a spaniel, the crew
had also saved from the wreck, were the only
ones known to LEE Boo; the sheep, goats,
and other cattle, therefore, which he met with
at Macao, were novelties that greatly excited

his surprise. The newfoundland dog, which had attracted so much notice, and become the property of his uncle Arra Kooker, being called *Sailor*, he applied that word to every animal which had four legs; so that, seeing some horses, he called them, *Clow Sailor*, that is *Great Sailor*. The next morning, observing a man on horseback pass the house, he was himself so wonderfully astonished, that he wanted every one to go out, and see the strange sight too. He afterwards went to the stables where the horses were: he felt, and stroked them, and was very inquisitive to know what their food was, as he had found they would not eat oranges, of which he had offered them some he had in his pocket. He was easily persuaded to mount one of them; and, on being informed what a noble, docile, and useful animal it was, he with great solicitude besought Captain Wilson to get one sent to his uncle, Raa Kook to whom he was sure it would be of great service.

G

The crew were waiting at Macao for a permit and boats to carry them to Canton, when Captain Churchill, of the Walpole, arriving, was so obliging as to accommodate them with a passage up to Whampoa; the chief mate, and five or six of the men only remaining with the Oroolong at Macao, till she should be sold.

LEE Boo found sufficient matter to keep his attention awake on board the Walpole; the furniture, chairs, tables, lamps, the upright bulk-heads, and deck over head, were all surprising. After silently casting his eyes over these objects, he whispered to Captain Wilson, that *clow ship* was *house*. It is to be supposed, that nothing on board the Walpole escaped his notice, as it was evident nothing on shore did. At Canton, being at the Company's table at the Factory, his admiration was much excited by the vessels of glass, of various shapes and sizes, particular the branches for holding candles. Having surveyed the numerous attendants behind the gentlemen's chairs,

as well as the variety of provisions and liquors,
he remarked to Captain Wilson, that " the
" king his father lived in a manner very differ-
" ent, having only a little fish, yam, or cocoa-
" nut, which he ate from off a leaf, and drank
" out of the shell of the nut, and, when his meal
" was finished, wiped his mouth and his fingers
" with a bit of cocoa-nut husk ; whereas the
" company present ate a bit of one thing, and
" then a bit of another, the servants always
" supplying them with a different plate, and
" different sorts of vessels to drink out of."
He seemed to relish tea from the first: coffee
he refused, as he did not like the smell of it,
yet at the same time saying, " he would drink
" it, if Captain Wilson ordered him." An
incident at Macao gave him an aversion to all
kinds of spirits. One of the seamen being
much intoxicated, LEE BOO supposing him
very ill, in great concern, applied to Mr.
Sharpe to relieve him. On being informed
of the nature of is ailment, that it is was the

effect of a liquor, in which common people
were too apt to indulge, and would soon go
off of itself, though it always injured the health,
and often was the cause of men's becoming
wicked, his anxiety subsisted;—but he would
never afterwards even taste spirits, saying,
when offered any, " it was not drink fit for a
" good and sensible man." Indeed, as to
eating and drinking, he observed great tem-
perance in both. How quick was the light of
wisdom and virtue kindled in the breast of
this young man!—Upon the first intimation, he
instantly conceived the pernicious effects of
drinking spirits, and resolved to guard himself against so vile a habit—There is scarcely
a trait in his character, but gives a proof of
correct judgment, or a striking lesson of
morality

The vessel having been sold at Macao,
Mr. Benger, and the men who remained with
him, accompanied by Mr. M'Intyre, went up
to Canton in one of the country boats. When

they arrived there, LEE Boo happening to be
at breakfast near a window, which looked towards the water, the instant he caught a distant view of them, without uttering a syllable
to any one, he sprang from his seat, and was
at the edge of the river, before the boat reached the shore: he received them with the utmost eagerness and joy, shook their hands with
the warmest expressions of affection, and manifested the greatest impatience to get them into
the house, fearing that from their staying behind, they had not fared so well as himself.

During LEE Boo's stay at Canton, several
gentlemen, who had been at Madagascar, and
some other places, where the throwing of the
spear is practised, and who had themselves a
considerable degree of skill in the art, expressed a desire of seeing him perform this exercise; and a meeting was appointed at the hall
of the Factory for the purpose. LEE Boo
did not at first point his spear to any particular
object, but only shook and poised it, as is

usual before throwing it from the hand. This
the gentlemen also were able to do. But it
being proposed to aim at some particular
point, they fixed upon a gauze cage, which
hung up in the hall, and had a bird painted
in the middle, as their mark. LEE Boo took
up his spear with much seeming indifference,
levelled at the little bird, and struck it through
the head, to the amazement of all his competitors,
who, at the great distance whence they flung,
could not without much difficulty hit even the
cage.—This is a proof of the wonderful effect
of habit and practice. The spear is a weapon
in use among most uncivilized nations, not acquainted with fire-arms, whose constant exercise from childhood to manhood is the throwing of it, in which they acquire a degree of
skill, which sets all competition at defiance.
Early and constant application, therefore, is
the natural means by which excellence is to be
attained in every thing.

LEE Boo was much delighted with the

stone buildings, and spacious rooms of the
houses at Canton: the flat ceilings, however,
still continued to be marvellous in his eyes; he
often compared them with the sloping thatched
roofs at Pelew, and said, " that by the time
" he went back, he should have learnt how it
" was done, and would then tell the people
" there, in what manner they ought to build."
In all his observations, the grand consideration
he seemed to have at heart was, the advantage
and improvement of his country.

Among the things brought in for tea, at the
house of Mr. Freeman, one of the Company's
Agents, was a sugar-dish of blue glass, which
greatly striking LEE Boo's fancy, that gentleman was induced, when tea was over, to
take him into another room where there were
two barrels of the same kind of blue glass
(holding about two quarts each) placed on
brackets; the alluring colour again caught his
eye; he gazed at them with much eagerness—
went away—returned to them with new delight.

Mr. Freeman, observing to what excess he was captivated by these articles, told him he would make him a present of them, and that he should carry them to Pelew. This threw him into such an ecstacy, that he could scarcely contain himself: he declared, that on his return, Abba Thulle should possess so great a treasure; and he wished his relations could but have a view of them; he was sure they would be lost in astonishment at the sight.

Captain Wilson now laid before his companions in adverse fortune, a statement of what the sale of the ship, stores, &c. had produced, and divided the whole in equal shares among them. This done, he acquainted them, that they were at liberty to provide for themselves as opportunity should offer, yet recommended to them all, but particularly his officers, to return to England, where, he had no doubt, they would in some measure, be recompensed for the hardships they had undergone, by the Honourable Company, to whom, he said, he

should duly represent (what he felt himself in
the highest degree obliged to them for) the
good order, unanimity, and excellent conduct
they had presevered in, throughout the trying
scenes they had experienced together, which
had afforded them an opportunity of so zea-
lously testifying their regard for the general
service.

Mr. Sharp, to whose immediate care, as has
been mentioned, LEE Boo was committed on
leaving Oroolong, now resigned his charge to
Captain Wilson, and came home in the Lascelles Indiaman, Captain Wakefield; the other
officers and men engaged in different ships, as
vacancies occurred: but the greater part of the
latter embarked in the York, Captain Blanchard.
As may be conceived, these partners in distress
did not separate without feelings of concern
and regret.

Captain Wilson and his charge embarked
in the Morse Indiaman, Captain Joseph Elliott,
who, in the most friendly manner, accommo-

dated them with a passage to England,
Throughout the whole voyage, LEE BOO was
treated by that gentleman with much kindness
and attention, and was himself so good hu-
moured and agreeable, that every one was
ready to render him any service in his power.—
Every ship the Morse met with at sea LEE
Boo must needs know the name of: he would
repeat what he was told over and other, till he
had fixed it well in his memory; and, as each
inquiry was gratified, he made a knot in his
line: but time multiplied these knots so greatly, that he was obliged to repeat his remarks
every day to refresh his memory, in doing
which he was often under the necessity of
applying to Captain Wilson or others, on
forgetting the circumstance any particular knot
referred to. The officers in the Morse, with
whom only he associated, when they saw him
thus employed with his line, used to say, he
was *reading his journal*. He frequently in-
quired after all the people in the Oroolong,

who had gone on board different ships at
China, particularly a son of the Captain's, who
was one of them, and Mr. Sharp.

Lee Boo had been but a short time on the
voyage, when he requested Captain Wilson to
get him a book, and point out to him the letters, that he might learn to read: the Captain
kindly embraced every convenient opportunity
of gratifying this wish, and had the satisfaction of discovering great readiness of apprehension in his young pupil.

On arriving at St. Helena, our young voyager was much struck with the soldiers and
cannon on the fortifications: and four English
men of war coming in soon afterwards, afforded him a sight highly delightful, especially as
some of them had two tiers of guns. It was
explained to him, that this sort of ships are
intended only for fighting, and that the others,
which he then saw in the bay, were for com-
mercial purposes, and transported the produce
and manufactures of one country to another,

Captain Buller, the commander of the
Chaser, politely took him on board his own,
and another ship, in order that he might see
the men exercise at the great guns and small
arm: a sight, with which his imaginations
was exceedingly impressed.

On being taken to a school, he expressed a
wish that he could learn like the boys, feeling,
as he did, his deficiency in knowledge.—The
truant would do well to compare his own
opinion of schools with those of LEE Boo,
who, regarding them as affording the means
of instruction and improvement, considered
them as highly beneficial, and felt the strong-
est desire to attend them: whereas, the idler,
thinking only of the tasks which he has to
learn, sees not the advantages to be reaped there,
but looks upon them with disgust, as places of
drudgery and punishment, and consequently
seeks to avoid them. Let him blush and
learn better notions from an untutored native
of Pelew.

He desired, and was permitted to ride on
horseback into the country: he sat well, and
galloped without the least fear of falling, and
appeared highly gratified both with the novelty and pleasure of the exercise.

In the Company's garden, he remarked some
shady walks, formed with bamboos arching
over head on lattice-work, and was struck
with the refreshing coolness they afforded.
He observed, " that the people on this island
" had but little wood, yet applied it to a good
" purpose; whereas his own countrymen were
" ignorant of the advantages they might enjoy,
" having a great abundance, but not knowing
" in what manner to use it. When he went
" back, he said, he would speak to the king
" tell him how defective they were, and have
" men set to work on such bowers as he had
" seen."

Such was the dawn of illumination in LEE
Boo's mind! He felt his ignorance, and had
the good sense to catch at every thing, which

might lead him forward to information and improvement.

At St. Helena, he had the happiness of an interview with his first friend Mr. Sharp, who arrived at that island in the Lascelles before he quitted it. He first saw him from a window, and ran out with extreme impatience to take him by the hand, shewing by his manner, the gratitude he felt for the kind attention that gentleman had shewn him.

As the Morse drew near the British Channel, the number of vessels, pursuing their different courses, increased so much, that LEE BOO was obliged to give up keeping his journal; however, he still continued very inquisitive to know whither they were sailing. When the ship reached the Isle of Wight, Captain Wilson, his brother, the Prince, and several other passengers, left her, and taking a boat, arrived safe at Portsmouth the 14th of July, 1784. When landed, the variety of houses, the ramparts, and the number and size of the men of

war then in the harbour, rivetted LEE Boo's
attention; he was so totally wrapped up in
wonder, that he had no recollection even to
ask any questions.

The officer of the Morse, charged with the
dispatches, being about to repair immediately
to London, Captain Wilson naturally impa-
tient to behold his family, accompanied him,
entrusting LEE Boo to the care of his brother,
both of whom were to follow in a coach which
was to set off in the evening. As soon as he
arrived in town, he was carried to Captain
Wilson's house at Rotherhithe, where, as may
be supposed, he was not a little happy in re-
joining his adopted father, and being introduced
to his family.

Part of his journey from Portsmouth, passed
during the night: the return of day, however,
brought full employment for his eyes; and
he reached what was to be, for some time his
home, in all the natural glow of his youthful
spirits. Whatever he had observed in silence,

was now eagerly disclosed. He described the
circumstances of his journey; said it had been
very pleasant, that he had been put into a
little house, which was run away with by
horses—that he slept, but still was going on;
and whilst he went one way, the fields, houses,
and trees, all went another; every thing, from
the quickness of travelling, appearing to be in
motion.

When, at the hour of rest, he was conducted
to his chamber, he saw, for the first time, a
four-post bed. Scarcely could he conceive
what it meant—he jumped in and jumped out
again—felt and pulled aside the curtains—got
into bed, and then got out a second time, to
admire its outward form. At length, when he was
fully acquainted with its use and convenience,
he laid himself down to sleep, saying, that
in England there was a house for every thing.

About a week after his arrival in this country, he accompanied Captain Wilson to dine
with a party at a friend's where he first met

George Keate, Esq. the gentleman, who has
with so much ability written the account at large
of the Pelew Islands: LEE BOO was then
master of but very little English, yet, between
words and actions, contrived to make himself
pretty well understood, and seemed to com-
prehend the greater part of what was said to
him, especially when explained by the Captain.
He wore his hair in the fashion of his own country, was of a middling stature, and had a countenance so strongly marked with sense and
good humour, as instantly to prepossess every
one in his favour, and moreover enlivened by
eyes so quick and intelligent, that they might
truly be said to tell his thoughts without the
aid of language. Though Mr. Keate's expec-
tations had been greatly raised by the accounts
he had previously received of this new man, as
he was called at Macao, yet, when that gentleman had been a little time in his company, he
was perfectly astonished at the ease and gen-
tleness of his manners. But it would be best

here to let Mr. Keate speak in his own person.
" He was," says he, " lively and pleasant,
" and had a politeness without form or res-
" traint, which appeared to be the result of
" natural good breeding. As I chanced to
" sit near him at table, I paid him a great
" deal of attention, which he seemed to be
" very sensible of. Many questions were of
" course put to Captain Wilson by the company,
" concerning this personage, and the country
" he had brought him from, which no Euro-
" pean had ever visited before: he obligingly
" entered on many particular circumstances,
" which were highly interesting, spoke of the
" battles in which his people had assisted the
" king of Pelew, and of the peculiar manner
" the natives had of tying up their hair when
" going to war: LEE BOO, who fully under-
" stood what his friend was explaining, very
" obligingly, and unasked, untied his own,
" and threw it into the form Captain Wilson
" had been describing.—I might tire the rea-

" der, were I to mention all the trifling oc-
"·currences of a few hours, rendered only of
" consequence, from the singularity of this
" young man's situation; suffice it to say, there
" was in all his actions, such affability, and
" propriety of behaviour, that, when he took
" 'eave of the company, there was hardly one
" present who did not feel a satisfaction in
" having had an interview with him."

" I went to Rotherhithe," continues Mr.
Keate, " a few days after, to see Captain
" Wilson. LEE Boo was reading at a win-
" dow; he recollected me instantly, and flew
" with eagerness to the door to meet mè,
" looked on me as a friend, and ever after,
" attached himself to me, appearing to be
" happy whenever we met together. In this
" visit, I had a good deal of conversation with
" him, and we mutually managed to be pretty
" well understood by each other; he seemed
" to be pleased with every thing about him;
" and said, *All fine country, fine street, fine*

" coach, *and house upon house up to sky*,
" putting alternately one hand above another,
" by which I found (their own habitations
" being all on the ground) that he at that time,
" considered every separate story of our build-
" ings as a distinct house."

This promising young man was introduced
to several of the Directors of the India Company, taken on visits to many of the Captain's
friends, and gradually shewn most of the
public buildings in the metropolis; but Captain Wilson very prudently avoided taking
him to any of the places of public entertain-
ment, for fear of his catching the small-pox, a
distemper, for which it was proposed to ino-
culate him, as soon as he should become sufficiently acquainted with the English language,
to be made fully sensible of the necessity of
the measure: for it was judged, and surely
not without good reason, that to bring upon
him so troublesome and offensive a disease,
without first explaining its nature, and pre-

paring his mind to submit to it, might weaken
that unlimited confidence he had placed in his
adopted father.

Lee Boo's attention was always alive to
every thing that passed, and it was evident,
from his questions, that his chief desire was
to collect information which might be useful to
his countryman. One day, as he and Captain
Wilson were walking through the streets of
London, they saw some men at a distance,
carrying what appeared to be a dead body,
and on enquiring they learned, that a boatman
had fallen into the river Thames, and not
knowing how to swim, had sunk to the bottom;
but that his comrades, having found the body
after a long search, were then taking it to a
neighbouring house, to try the means which
are recommended for the recovery of drowned
persons. This was enough to raise the tender-
est pity in the young Prince. He did not,
indeed, know the meaning of all he heard—
since in Pelew the natives are taught to swim

from their infancy, and therefore such acci-
dents seldom occur; and besides, he could not
understand how it was possible to bring back
to life, a person who is to all appearance
dead, when the body having lain in the water
for a long time is become stiff and cold, when
the eyes are closed, and the heart no longer
beats. He could perceive, however, that a
fellow creature had met with a misfortune, and
therefore entreated Captain Wilson's permission to assist in relieving him. Afraid of the
danger he must run of catching the small pox,
his friend could not grant his request, but he
promised to enquire after the poor man, and
also to explain to him fully, the manner in
which persons who seem to be dead from
drowning, are to be treated. After dinner,
therefore, Captain Wilson took an opportunity
of satisfying his curiosity, because it arose from
a humane desire of doing good. When Captain Wilson had explained to Lee Boo, he
looked down at his own breast, and though,

like many other boys, he had never thought of
it, he now saw at once, that the rising and
working of his chest was caused by the air he
drew in, or drove out by his mouth, and that
by the mode recommended, breathing could
be exactly imitated.

During the explanation, which LEE BOO
never interrupted, except to ask the meaning
of a few words he did not understood, his
countenance shewed how deeply he felt inter-
ested in what he heard. "And now, said
Captain Wilson, in concluding his account, I
must add, that the country you have been sent
to by your kind father Abba Thulle, is not
less remarkable for the humanity of its people,
than for the many improvements which have
so often astonished you. A number of good
men have joined together, for the purpose of
endeavouring to recover all persons who may
have been taken lifeless out of the water, and
for making known the best and simplest means
to be used in such cases; they call themselves

the *Humane Society*, and print and circulate
little books, containing the necessary directions;
they have a house upon the banks of the river
Thames, where drowned persons may be
taken, and where people are constantly ready
to assist in their recovery—and they even give
rewards in money, or a silver medal to all who
have either plunged into the water to save a
drowning person, or assisted in the endeavours
used to retsore him to life."

The rest of that evening, LEE Boo passed
in his own room—it seemed to be a principle
of duty with this young man, to allow himself
no self indulgence to stand in the way of his
improvement. He therefore denied himself
the pleasure of seeing the family, that he might
imprint on his memory every thing he had
heard from Captain Wilson.

After being somewhat habituated to the
manners of this country, he went every day to
an academy at Rotherhithe, for the purpose of
being instructed in reading and writing. His

application was equal to his great desire of
learning; and he conducted himself there with
such propriety, and in a manner so engaging,
that he gained not only the esteem of the gentleman under whose tuition he was placed, but
also the affection of his young companions—
which should ever be a main object with
youth at school. When he returned to his
home, each day he diverted all his family by
his vivacity, noticing every singularity he had
observed in any of his school-fellows, and with
great good humour, imitating and taking them
off; sometimes he added, that he would have
a school of his own when he returned to Pelew,
and should be thought very wise when he
taught the great people their letters.

In addressing Mr. Wilson, he always called
him *Captain;* but would never address Mrs.
Wilson (for whom he had the most affectionate regard) by any other appellation than
mother, considering *that* the most respectfu
term he could use. Being often told he should

say Mrs. Wilson, his constant answer was, *No, no mother, mother.*

Wherever LEE BOO was, his observation extended to every thing around him, having an ardent desire for information, which he always received with thanks. Upon noticing any new effect, he always expressed a wish to know the cause. A young lady, who happened to be one day in company where he was, sat down to an harpsichord, to observe in what manner he would be affected by music. He seemed greatly surprised so find so much sound proceed from it : the instrument was opened, to let him see its interior construction he pored over it with much curiosity, took particular notice of the motion of the jacks, and shewed far greater inclination to discover the means by which the sounds were produced, than to attend to the music itself. A Pelew song was afterwards requested of him; he waited not for repeated entreaties, as singers usually do, but began one immediately. How-

ever, in his great exertions, his breast laboured
extremely, his whole countenance changed,
and his tones were so harsh and discordant,
that every one's ears were stunned. Yet
after some residence in this country, he readily
caught two or three English songs, in which
his voice by no means seemed unmusical.

He was of a very mild and compassionate
disposition : and various instances proved
he had brought from Pelew, that spirit of
benevolence and humanity which our countrymen found so much to prevail there.
Nevertheless, he was at all times actuated by
judgment and discretion—if he met with
young beggars, he rebuked as well as the little
English he knew would permit; but he always
yielded to the entreaties of old age—*Must give
poor old man*, he would say—*old man no able
to work.*

Lee Boo, becoming much disgusted with
Boyam his servant, who turned out to be an
unprincipled fellow, solicited Captain Wilson

to send him back to Sumatra: (the country
of the Malays,) and Tom Rose (mentioned before as interpreter on the part of the English,
in conversing with the natives of Pelew), a
person of tried fidelity, and who had picked
up a good deal of the Pelew language, being
now in England, was appointed in his room,
greatly to the satisfaction of the prince.

Captain Wilson was now and then indisposed
with severe head-aches, which obliged him to
lie down upon the bed for relief. The feelings
of LEE Boo were ever sensibly affected on
these occasions; he was always anxious and
unhappy; he would creep up softly to his
guardian's chamber, and for a long time together sit silent and motionless by his bed-side,
only now and then peeping gently between
the curtains, to see if he slept or lay easy.

During the voyage to China, LEE Boo
naturally contracted an intimacy with Captain
Wilson's son, who was a few years younger
than himself, and of very amiable manners.

This intimacy ripened under the father's roof,
to strong mutual attachment. It may be said,
they looked upon one another as brothers:
and LEE Boo, in the hours of retirement from
his school pursuits, could not but be happy to
have such a companion to converse with, to
exercise the throwing of the spear, or partake
in any innocent amusement. The two friends
had so much indulged themselves one morning
in their diversion with the spear, that a message
of a particular nature, with which Captain
Wilson had charged his son, was totally for-
gotten. Upon inquiry after dinner, the Captain discovered the neglect: and being hurt
at it, chid his son for his fault, telling him he
was idle and careless. From the tone of voice
with which this reproof was uttered, LEE Boo
conceived and felt the anger of the father, and
slipped unobserved out of the room. The
matter was immediately dropped and another
subject started. Presently LEE Boo was
missed, and his companion, who was sent to

look for him, found him in a back room quite
dejected.   On being desired to return to the
family, he took his young friend by the hand,
and entering the parlour, went up to the
father, laid hold of his hand, joined it with
that of his son, and pressing them together,
dropped over both those tears which his affectionate heart could not on the occasion sup-
press.—Would to God that those who have
been taught from Heaven that " Blessed are
" the peace-makers," would *go and do like* this
unenlightened child of nature!

Lee Boo dining with a party of friends at
Mr. Keate's, in the course of conversation, that
gentleman asked what effect painting had upon
him; when one of the company, Dr. Carmichael Smyth, wished Mr. Keate to bring a
miniature of himself, that all might observe
how he was struck by it. The prince had
no sooner taken it in his hand, than darting
his eyes to the right object, he called out
Misser Keat,—very nice, very good. Captain

Wilson then asked him, if he understood what
it signified. His answer was, LEE Boo *understand well—that Misser Keat die—this Misser
Keate live.*—Mr. Keate well observes of this
little sentence, that a long discourse on portrait
painting could not better have explained its
utility and intent.

Mrs. Wilson, happening to sit opposite to
LEE Boo at table, desired him to help her to
some cherries. He was about to take them up
with his fingers; but Mrs. Wilson pleasantly
noticing it to him, he instantly made use of a
spoon. A blush, however, with which his
countenance was immediately covered, shewed
very visibly, even through his dark complex-
ion, the sense he entertained of the small breach
of politeness he had been guilty of.

Another lady of the same party, being near
fainting from the heat of the weather, was
constrained to quit the room. Our amiable
prince was greatly distressed at the incident;
and, when at tea-time the lady again made

her appearance, his inquiries and particular attention to her, manifested alike his tenderness and good breeding.

He preferred riding in a coach to any other mode of conveyance; because he said, at the same time, that people were carried where they wished to go, they could sit very commodiously, and converse together.

Lee Boo derived particular pleasure from going to church, where, though he did not understand the words of the service, yet he perfectly comprehended the intent of it; he always behaved with the greatest attention and reverence. Once, when Captain Wilson told him, that saying prayers at church was to make men good, that, when they died and were buried, they might live again above, pointing to the sky, Lee Boo answered with much earnestness—*All same Pelew—bad men stay in earth—good men go into sky—become very beautiful*, holding his hand in the air, and giving a fluttering motion to his fingers—

thereby explaining, his countrymen's belief of
the existence of the spirit, after the death of
the body.

In order to avoid the small-pox, as already
mentioned, and also to prevent his mind from
being disturbed, and drawn off from the
attainment of the English language, the great
means by which information was to be conveyed to him, Captain Wilson was very cautious,
and sparing in letting him go abroad; however,
he not only generally accompanied the Captain on visits to friends, but had also a view of
most of the public buildings in the metropolis,
the river, shipping, and bridges, which struck
him greatly; he was, moreover, several times
gratified with seeing the Guards exercised in
St. James's Park, as every thing of a military
kind greatly engaged his attention.

There was something very singular in
Lee Boo's opinion of the art of ascending
in the air in a balloon, which so much engrossed
the notice of the people of this country, at the

time of his coming here. It was given in conversation with his friend Mr. Keate, whose words
we shall quote in laying it before the reader.

"I went to see him," says that gentleman,
"the morning after Lunardi's first ascent in
"the balloon, not doubting but that I should
"have found him in the greatest degree asto-
"nished at an exhibition which had excited
"so much curiosity, even amongst ourselves;
"but to my great surprise, it did not appear
"to have engaged him in the least. He said,
"*he thought it a very foolish thing to ride in
"*the air like a bird, when a man could travel
"*so much more pleasantly on horseback, or in a
"*coach.*—He was either not aware," adds
Mr. Keate, "of the difficulty or hazard of the
"enterprize, or it is not improbable, that a
"man flying up through the clouds, suspen-
"ded at a balloon, might have been ranked by
"him as a common occurrence, in a country
"which was perpetually spreading before him
"so many objects of surprise."

Whenever he had an opportunity of viewing
gardens, the plants and fruit-trees excited his
particular attention: he would make many
inquiries concerning them, saying, when he
should return home, he would carry with him
seeds of such as would grow in Pelew. He
frequently used to talk of the things he should
then persuade the king, his father to alter or
adopt; and his principal researches were directed to the discovery of whatever might
prove beneficial to his country.

This inquisitive and pains-taking young man
was proceeding extremely fast in gaining the
English language, and making so rapid a progress with his pen, that in a short time he
would have written a very fine hand, when,
alas! he was attacked by that very disease
against which so much caution had been used.

On the 16th of December, he found himself
greatly disordered, and in the course of a day
or two an eruption appeared all over him.
Captain Wilson, full of apprehension, had im-

mediate recourse to Dr. Carmichael Smyth, whom we have before mentioned, requesting him to see the prince. That gentleman kindly attended, and upon the first sight of him, not only pronounced the distemper to be the small-pox, but was obliged to add the melancholy information that the appearances were such as almost totally precluded the hope of recovery. However, the Doctor ordered what was then necessary, and, on Captain Wilson's earnestly soliciting the continuance of his visits, assured him, that, however inconvenient the distance, he would not fail daily to attend the issue of the disease.

In this sad condition, the afflicted youth was deprived of the solacing presence of his dear friend Captain Wilson, who not having had the small pox himself, yielded to the entreaties of his family not to go into his chamber. However, his first and faithful friend Mr. Sharp, on hearing of his illness, repaired to his assistance, nor quitted the Captain's house, till it was become the scene of death!

house, till it was become the scene of death !
—However much our suffering prince regret-
ted the loss of the Captain's company, yet,
when informed of the reason and necessity of
his absence, he could not but acquiesce in it,
anxiously inquiring from time to time concerning his health, full of dread, lest he should
catch the disorder, as he still continued in the
house.

During the progress of this grievous distemper, LEE Boo maintained the utmost firm-
ness of mind, and, having the highest opinion
of Dr. Smyth, never refused to take any thing
administered to him, when informed that he
desired it.—The youthful reader is here particularly called upon to imitate poor LEE Boo,
in cases of like necessity.

Hearing of an indisposition which now happened to Mrs. Wilson, and confined her to her
bed, LEE Boo instantly took alarm, exclaim-
ing, *what mother ill*, LEE Boo *get up to see
her !* He actually did so, and would go to

K

her apartment to be sure how she really was.
—On the Thursday before his death, as he
walked across the room, he looked at himself
in the glass, and finding his face much swoln
and disfigured, and covered, as well as his
whole body, with sores, shook his head, and in
seeming disgust with his own appearance, turned
away, telling Mr. Sharp that *his father and
mother much grieve, for they knew he was very
sick.* This he several times repeated.   In the
evening growing worse, he became sensible of
his danger; and taking Mr. Sharp by the
hand, and steadfastly fixing his eyes upon him,
said with great earnestness, *Good friend, when
you go to Pelew, tell Abba Thulle, that Lee
Boo take much drink to make small-pox go
away, but he die—that the Captain and Mother
(Mrs. Wilson) very kind—all English very good
men—was much sorry he could not speak to the
king, the number of fine things the English had
got.* He then enumerated the presents which
had been made him, and expressed his wishes

, that Mr. Sharp would distribute them, when he returned to Pelew, amongst the chiefs, recommending to his special care, the blue glass barrels on brackets, which he particularly directed to be given to the king.

His faithful servant Tom Rose, who stood at the foot of the bed, melted into tears at this melancholy scene: the agonized master gently rebuked him for his weakness, saying, *Why should he be crying so, because* LEE BOO *die?*

Whatever he felt, his spirits did not allow him to complain. Mrs. Wilson's chamber adjoined to his own, and he would often call out to inquire if she was better, always adding, to prevent her suffering any disquietude, on his account, *do well, Mother,* LEE BOO *do well.*

The small-pox not rising, after eight or nine days from its coming out, he began to feel himself sink, and told Mr. Sharp *he was going away.* What he suffered in the latter part of

K 2

his existence, was severe indeed : his mind,
however, continued perfectly clear and calm
to the last, and the strength of his consti-
tution struggled long and hard against the
violence of his disorder, till, overwhelmed
nature yielded in the contest.

His good friend Mr. Keate was kindly informed every day by Dr. Smyth, of the state
of his patient, and being under an engagement,
with his family, to pass a week with Mr. Brook
Watson, at Sheen, (who was alike anxious and
alarmed for this amiable young man,) he requested the Doctor to have the goodness, to continue
his information to him there.   Accordingly, two
days after he left town, he received from that
gentleman, an account of the melancholy issue,
which we cannot forbear laying before the
reader, in his own words.

"Monday, Dec. 27 , 1784.

"MY DEAR SIR,

"It is an unpleasant task for me to be the herald
of bad news ; yet, according to my promise, I must

inform you of the fate of poor LEE Boo, who died
this morning without a groan, the vigour of his mind
and body resisting to the very last.—Yesterday the
secondary fever coming on, he was seized with a
shivering fit, succeeded by head-ache, violent beating
of the heart, anxiety, and difficult breathing: he
again used the warm bath, which, as formerly, afforded him a temporary relief, he had a blister put on
his back, which was as ineffectual as those applied
to his legs. He expressed all his feelings to me in
the most forcible and pathetic manner, put my hand
upon his heart, leant his head on my arm, and explained his uneasiness in breathing; but when I was
gone, he complained no more, showing, that he complained with a view to be relieved, not to be pitied.—
In short, living or dying, he has given me a lesson,
which I shall never forget: and surely, for patience
and fortitude he was an example worthy of imitation!
—I did not see Captain Wilson when I called this
morning, but the maid servant was in tears, and
every person in the family wore the face of grief;
poor LEE Boo's affectionate temper made every
one look upon him as a brother or a son.—I make no
doubt, Mr Watson and his family will all join in re-
gretting the untimely end of our poor prince. From

you, my friend, something more will be expected;
and, though you cannot bring him back to life, you
are called upon particularly, (considering his great
attachment to you,) not to let the memory of so much
virtue pass away unrecorded.—But I am interrupted
in these melancholy reflections, and have only time
to assure you, of (what will never pass away but
with myself) the sincere friendship of your affectionate, &c.

> " *James Carmichael Smyth.*"

Captain Wilson, having notified to the
India House, the death of this admirable youth,
received orders to conduct his funeral with
every mark of decency and respect. He was
accordingly interred in Rotherhithe church-
yard, attended by the Captain and his brother,
and such was the affectionate regard, which
all who knew entertained for him, that not
only the young people of the school, but even
the whole parish, assembled to see the last
ceremonies paid to his remains. An additional
honour was soon afterwards done him, by the

India Company's ordering a tomb to be erected over his grave, on which is the following inscription:

To the memory
of Prince LEE BOO,
A native of the Pelew or Palos Islands;
And son to Abba Thulle, rupack or king
of the Island Coorooraa
who departed this life on the 27th of December,
1784,
aged 20 years;
This stone is inscribed,
by the Honourable United East India Company,
as a testimony of esteem
for the humane and kind treatment afforded
by his father to the crew of their ship,
the Antelope, Captain Wilson,
which was wrecked off that island,
on the night of the 9th of August, 1783.

Stop, reader, Stop! let Nature claim a tear—
A prince of mine, LEE Boo lies buried here.

Mention has already been made of the presents consigned by LEE Boo, to the care of Mr. Sharp for his father and friends.

Amongst the other little property which the
lamented youth left behind, were found, carefully and separately put up, the stones or seeds
of most of the fruits he had tasted in England.
We have before remarked, that the benefit of
his country, seemed to be his ultimate aim in
all his observations; and here is a striking in-
stance, considering his abode with us was no
more than five months and twelve days, that,
amidst all the novelties which surrounded him,
he had duly given his attention to the object,
which, it is presumed, had been particularly
recommended to it, previous to his departure
from Pelew.

We shall conclude this little book, with
Mr. Keate's reflections, upon the fate of the
excellent subject of it, in his own words, as too
interesting to be omitted, and too perfect to be
be altered or abridged without injury.

"From these trifling anecdotes, of this amiable
youth," says he, "cut off in the moment that his character began to blossom, what hopes might not have
been entertained of the future fruit such a plant

would have produced.—He had both ardour and talents for improvement, and every gentle quality of the heart to make himself belóved ; so, that as far as the dim sight of mortals is permitted to penetrate, he might, had his days been lengthened, have *carried back* to his own country—not the *vices* of a new world—but those *solid* advantages, which his own good sense would have suggested, as likely to become most useful to it.

" But how *carry back?* That event depended not on himself; a naked, *confiding* stranger, he trusted implicitly to others, and left the protecting arms of a father without apprehension—without conditions.—The evening before the Oroolong sailed, the king asked Captain Wilson, how long it might be before his return to Pelew ? and being told that it would probably be about thirty moons, or might chance to extend to six more, Abba Thulle, drew from his basket, a piece of *line*, and after making thirty knots on it, a little distance from each other, left a long space, and then adding six others, carefully put it by.

" As the slow but sure steps of Time have been moving onward, the reader's imagination, will figure the anxious parent, resorting to this cherished remembrancer, and with joy untying the earlier records of each elapsing period ; as he sees him advancing on his *line*, he will conceive the joy redoubled;—a when nearly approaching to the *thirtieth* knot, almost accusing the planet of the night, for passing so tardily away.

" When verging towards the termination of his latest reckoning, he will then picture his mind, glowing with parental affection, occasionally alarmed by doubt, yet still buoyed up by hope,—he will fancy him pacing inquisitively the sea-shore, and often commanding his people to ascend every rocky height, and glance their eyes along the level line of the horizon, which bounds the surrounding ocean, to see if haply it might not, in some part, be broken by the distant appearance of a returning sail.

" Lastly, he will view the good Abba Thulle, wearied out by that expectation, which so many returning moons since his reckoning *ceased*, have by this time taught him, he had nourished in vain.— But the reader will bring him back to his remembrance, as armed with that unshaken fortitude, that was equal to the trials of varying life.—After some allowance for natural grief, he will suppose him placidly resigned to the will of Providence.

" Should this not be absolutely the case of our friendly king—as the human mind is far more pained by *uncertainty* than a knowledge of the *worst*— every reader will lament, he should remain ignorant, that his long-looked-for son can return no more !"

POSTSCRIPT.

There are very few young persons, whom the preceding narrative has brought acquainted with LEE BOO, but regret that Providence denied him a return to his native country: until that fatal disorder, the small-pox, seized him, every reader was, no doubt, picturing to himself, the happiness which LEE BOO's arrival at Pelew would give to his excellent father, Abba Thulle—the improvements he would introduce, amongst an innocent and benevolent people, and, the joy his own feeling heart would experience at being the instrument of so much good to his countrymen.—But, these scenes were never to be realized, other hands than his were to present the little presents he had so carefully packed up for his friends, and other eyes to witness the growth or failure of the seeds which he intended to plant on his return.

In conformity to the wish expressed by Mr. Keate, the Directors of the East India Company, resolved to send out vessels to acquaint the king with the death of his son, and orders were sent to Bombay, to equip two for that purpose. Accordingly, the Panther and the Endeavour sailed on 24th of August, 1790, having on board two officers who had been shipwrecked along with Captain Wilson.

.. The southernmost of Pelew islands, was in sight on the 21st, and on the 22nd, the vessels came to an anchor within two miles of the shore. In the evening a number of canoes were observed rowing very fast, and one of them had a great number of paddles. This was known to be the king's canoe. He received the account of his son's death with fortitude, saying, he never entertained any doubt of the goodness of the English, and Captain Wilson, who he was sure, would cherish him. He was greatly disappointed at not seeing the Captain, but appeared satisfied that he was alive and well, and promoted to the command of a much larger vessel than the Antelope. The two officers, Lieutenants Wedgeborough and White, were immediately recognized by the natives, and experienced the most affectionate reception from them.

FINIS.

Plummer and Brewis, Printers, Love Lane, Eastcheap.

CPSIA information can be obtained
at www.ICGtesting.com
Printed in the USA
LVHW032104290122
709581LV00001B/8